How to Become an Expert at Writing eBooks

Entrepreneur Book Series

Colvin Nyakundi

Mendon Cottage Books

JD-Biz Publishing

Disclaimer

The information in this book is provided for informational purposes only and it is not intended for use as a substitute for proper financial or legal direction by a qualified financial or legal advisor. The information is believed to be accurate as presented based on research by the author.

No claims of income are given and examples are used to portray the ideas of the author as possibilities without representing actual earnings that can be made.

The author or publisher is not responsible for financial loss or damage incurred by implementing ideas mentioned in this book. The author or publisher is not responsible for errors or omissions that may exist.

Warning

The Book is for informational purposes only and before starting or running any business, it is recommended that you consult with your financial or legal professional. Always follow all laws and regulations regarding taxes, selling, buying, or ecommerce.

Table of Contents

Introduction

The number of people writing e-books has increased tremendously over the past few decades. Some people manage to write several e-books while others write one or maybe two books only. Even those who've published several books still find it quite hard to maintain high quality standards while at the same time achieving their objectives. Have you ever wondered why some people become successful e-book authors while others aren't successful?

Some people also find it quite easy to get ideas on the title and topics to write about while others find it hard to do so. Even if you know what you want to write about, you might still find it difficult to get sources of information about the topic. If you're keen on becoming an expert at writing e-books, there are several things you have to know. You must know where you're going to get information pertaining to that book, how you'll get that information and how you'll use the information to write the e-book. All successful e-book authors also have to be capable of handling the logistical challenges involved in writing e-books.

If you're so much interested in becoming a successful e-book author, you need to start by reading the book "How to Become an Expert at writing e-Books." This book contains everything you'll need in order to start writing an e-book about anything. After you're through with reading this book, you'll know the kind of topic(s) you should write about.

This book is also equipped with guidelines on how to maintain high quality standards in all your e-books. You'll also learn about some of the mistakes that you should never make while writing an e-book.

Start your journey to becoming a professional e-book writer by reading the book "How to Become an Expert at writing e-Books."

Identifying the Title and Topics

Have you ever tried to write and publish any document? If you have, then you probably know that it is quite difficult to identify the best topic to write about. If you're not careful when selecting the topic, you might write a book that nobody will ever bother to read. You might also get bored midway and hence decide to abandon the whole project. This means that you'll have wasted a lot of your energy for no good reason.

Here are some of the things that should guide you when selecting the title of the e-book and the topics to include in the e-book:

- Target audience

Before you start writing the book, you need to ask yourself one simple but very important question: who is the book intended for? Is it meant to be read by the young generation, the older generation, parents, children, teachers, investors, politicians or for the general population?

If you carefully and accurately answer this question, you will find it quite easy to identify the title and topics to write about. Some people might be interested in some topics more than other people. For example, there are stories that could be so much interesting to children but pretty much boring to adults. On the other hand, romance novels are intended for adults and not children. If you live in a country whose majority population are Muslims, you probably won't write anything about the bible because most people won't be interested in reading it. It is therefore up to you to carefully evaluate your target audience before deciding the title of the e-book and the topics to include in the e-book.

- Why are you writing the book?

You also need to ask yourself why you're writing the e-book. Is it for entertainment, education, romance or a guide? If you know why you're writing the e-book, you will find it easier to figure out the general direction of the e-book. For example, entertainment and romance books tend to be more informal and are based on the writers own ideas. On the contrary, educational and guide books tend to be more formal and the author needs to do some research so as to write facts only. If you're thinking of writing an academic or guide e-book, you have to ensure that the titles and topics are helpful to the intended readers.

- Are you talented in the topics you want to write about?

One of the biggest mistakes you can ever do is start writing about something you're totally not interested or talented in. You may end up writing a very poor quality e-book with uncountable errors. When selecting the topic to write about, it is always advisable that you write about something you're talented in or like. For example, it is just not possible to write a book about football if you've never watched even a single football match or tournament. The only way you can write an objective e-book about something is if you're interested in the topic and are always willing to find out more information about the topic.

- Do you have the vigor to write the e-book?

Vigor is all about the energy and mindset required to write the e-book. Somebody with vigor is one who can be imaginative and write something very interesting about the topic. If you don't have the vigor to write the e-book, you might end up writing something so boring that nobody will read beyond the first few pages. You might be having the vigor to write about a given topic and not any other topic. The only way you can become a successful e-book author is if you identify the topics you can write about vigorously.

- Legal issues

It is any e-book author's wish that as many people as possible read his/her book. Some authors therefore would do anything to ensure that more people read the book. Some may decide to slander other people, give misleading information, include inaccurate facts or use other people's materials without their authorization. Even if you're trying to attract as many readers as possible, you should be careful not to land in jail. It is always advisable that you don't write about anything illegal or about something that somebody else would use to sue you. Try to include factual information and avoid any topic that may attract lawsuits. If possible, you should consult your lawyer to advice you on the topic that you should write about. The lawyer should also go through the e-book and make appropriate adjustments to topics that may attract lawsuits.

Sources of Information

The next step in writing an e-book involves the identification of the sources of information regarding the topic you want to write about. When contracted to write an e-book, you must ensure that you go through the sources of information recommended by the client. You should also always stick to the topics and titles approved by the client. If you're the one deciding what to write about, you just need to identify a topic that is widely covered and hence it is easy to find sources of information.

The following are some of the ways/places in which you can collect information about a given subject

- Modern trends

It is always advisable that you write about currently trending topics. The internet has totally revolutionized the way information is dispersed to the general population. Unlike in the past when there was no internet, it is now quite easy to find out what is happening anywhere in the world. As soon as something interesting happens, people will be interested in finding out more information about it. This means that they'll probably search it on the internet or even start reading books related to it. If you want your book to be read by many people, you must ensure that you always write about something that is trending. You can just search the internet for trending topics and then decide the tile and topics of the e-book.

- Social media platforms

The easiest way you can identify the most interesting topics is by looking at what your friends are posting on their walls in social media platforms such as Facebook, twitter or Whatsapp. After you've seen the kind of topics that interest most people, you can go ahead and write an e-book related to the topics.

- Current news

You can also gather ideas about the e-book by frequently watching news and noting topics that are frequently covered. You can also read newspaper articles and see the most common topics.

- Popular events in history

If you want to become a successful author, you must be an avid reader about all topics. Try reading about popular events in history and then see if you can write something about the event. For example you can write about the history of a great king or major discoveries in the modern world. You can also write about the history of a given country or area. In other words, there is so much to write about if you're interested in writing about major events in history.

- Writing about the future

Rather than waste so much information thinking of where to get information about an e-book, you can just write about the future. For example you can write about what you think is going to happen in the next few years or decade. Writing about the future is mostly suitable for authors with several publications and a good reputation. With a good reputation, more and more people will trust your ideas and hence they can easily purchase the book so as to see your take on the future.

- A library near your home

A library is also one of the best places to gather information if you're interested in writing an e-book. A standard library would have all types of books including academic books, novels, religious books and any other publication. One of the main advantages of gathering information in a library is that most hardcopy publications are normally authentic and contain well researched information. This is very different from collecting information from the internet as anybody can easily create a website and post any information that he/she wants. Before you quote information from any source, you can try and find out if it is approved or recommended by specialists in that area.

- Conducting interviews

You can also gather so much information by simply conducting online or face to face interviews. This method of collecting information is highly recommended if you want to write an e-book about current issues affecting the general population. For example, if you want to write an e-book about different climatic conditions in the world, you can conduct a research to establish how people feel when living in a particular climate. This way you won't have to visit a library and research about the characteristics of different climatic conditions in the world.

- Righting your thoughts

For you to become a successful author, you don't have to always write about other people's ideas. You can also decide to write down your thoughts about a given subject. If for example you're thinking of writing an e-book about relationships, you can just right your take on the subject. Just make sure you mention that the ideas listed in the e-book are your own personal opinions and not those of a professional. This way you'll be exonerating yourself from any liability that may arise in case the reader decides to implement the ideas listed in your book.

- Converting your personal diary into an book

If you've been filling your personal diary for the past couple of years, then you might want to convert it into an e-book. Using your personal diary as the source of information is very advantageous as you don't have to do a lot of research. All that you'll be doing is writing about the places you visited, the people you talked and the activities you were involved in.

How to Maintain High Quality

You might be thinking that it is easy to write an e-book but truth be told, it is not an easy task. Once you've written one high quality e-book, it is difficult to maintain high quality standards in all your subsequent e-books. The quality of an e-book is all about the words and phrases used in the e-book, how they're used and the general flow of the e-book. The message delivered by the e-book will also determine the quality of the e-book.

So as to maintain high quality standards when writing an e-book, you must ensure that you collect information from as many sources as possible. This way you'll minimize the probability of giving inaccurate information. By simply going through several sources of information, you'll also be able to see how other people delivered their message. This way you'll know several formats of writing e-books and hence choose one that is suitable for the topic you want to write about.

You must never start writing about anything without going through the source of information and understanding the concepts and ideas being put forward. After you've identified a potential source of information, the first thing you have to do is investigate its authenticity and accuracy of the information contained in the material. If for example you're reading something on the internet, you have to establish the qualifications of the author. You must also ensure that you get information from credible websites and not from those run by amateurs. Once you've verified the authenticity and accuracy of the information on the website, you can go ahead and skim the document so as to have an overview of what the document is talking about. The next phase involves reading the document keenly while noting down important points. These points will help you remember what to write when you start writing the book.

So as to maintain high quality standards, you must never plagiarize any material while writing an e-book. Plagiarism is the act of copying somebody else's work and presenting it as your own. Rather than copying and pasting somebody's work, you better read the document before writing what you've understood. It is important that you avoid using the exact words and phrases as used in the original document. If you have to use some words, phrases, paragraphs or pages, you need to contact the author and request the rights to use his/her document. Reading several sources of information before writing an e-book is one of the ways through which you can avoid plagiarizing somebody's work. Always keep in mind that plagiarism is an offence that is punishable by law. You can therefore be sued by the original author or any third party who owns the rights to the document you've copied.

Writing an e-book can sometimes be a tiring task, especially if you always write when you're too exhausted or in a hurry to do something else. If you're trying to write a given number of pages per day, you ought to be very careful so as not to use gibberish and filler words and statements. Gibberish words are words that are just unintelligible or stupid. They're characterized by incoherency and poor coordination of ideas. Once somebody reads your e-book, he/she will immediately notice when something isn't making any sense. Filler words are words that can be avoided by the author, but he/she chooses to deliberately include them in the e-book so as to increase the word-count. When filler words are excessively used in the e-book, it tends to be too long but with very few ideas being put forward. This means that the reader might be bored after reading the first few pages.

Contradictory statements should also be avoided by all possible means. A high quality e-book is one whose ideas agree with each other. You can avoid contradictory statements by doing thorough research on the subject and then deciding the direction to take. If there are divergent opinions about a given topic, you can always let the reader know the different opinions. You will then go ahead and state your own opinion and give reasons why you think your opinion is valid and why other people's opinions can be disregarded.

The message being conveyed in the e-book must not be ambiguous in any way. An ambiguous statement is one that is open to two or more interpretations. So as to avoid ambiguity, you must be very careful when selecting the words you use to convey a given message. In all languages, there are countless words and phrases with different meanings depending on the context they're being used. You must therefore use words that won't leave any doubt on the reader's mind about what you meant. So as to avoid ambiguity when writing an e-book, it is advisable that you let several people (from different backgrounds) go through the document before you publish it. You can then go ahead and enquire about what they learnt after reading the e-book. This way you'll know if the message you wrote is delivered just as you wanted.

Thorough editing of an e-book is also one of the ways through which you can maintain high quality standards. Human beings are subject to many errors in whatever activities they're involved in. Any author can therefore unknowingly make mistakes such as grammatical errors, spelling errors or repetition of key words and ideas. In order to minimize the probability of making an error, you should always write the e-book when you're not too tired or thinking of something else. You should also ensure that you're not nervous or anxious about anything. Just relax and write the e-book slowly in a quiet environment away from disturbances. You can also reduce the probability of making errors by hiring a proofreader or professional editor to go through the e-book and make the necessary adjustments.

You ought to mind your language when writing an e-book. This means that the words used in the e-book should not be offensive to your target audience. If for example you decide to use vulgar language in a book intended to be read by the general population, most people will probably not buy it or even read past the first few pages. Try to do some research about your target audience. Once you've ascertained the language frequently used by your target audience, you can then go ahead and use it in your book. You must avoid the use of slang language if the book is intended for use in official engagements or gatherings.

When writing a fiction e-book based on a true story, you must avoid using the actual names of the characters involved. Using their actual names puts you in an awkward position and you might end up being sued by the affected individual(s) for tarnishing their name(s). If you obtained information from an unauthorized source, you must protect the source of the information by not naming them in the book. This way you'll not endanger their lives or careers. If for example you're writing an e-book about a drug cartel, you should avoid using words, phrases or metaphors that might expose the identity of the person who supplied you with the information. Can you imagine what will happen if the cartel discovers the identity of the person who leaked information about them?

You can also ensure high quality standards by enhancing your creativity- even after doing research you still have to add something more so as to make the book more interesting. A high quality e-book requires a lot of creativity, imagination and the ability to come up with something new now and then.

You must also be highly motivated in order to write a high quality e-book. So as to be motivated, try to think of how much you're likely to gain once the book is published. You can sell the book and have some monetary gain. You could also be expanding your resume and hence increasing the probability of getting a better job or being promoted at work. If you're highly motivated when writing a given e-book, there is absolutely no way you can fail to maintain high quality standards.

What to Do When Writing E-Books

Writing an e-book may take several days, weeks or even months-depending on the number of chapters and the number of pages in each chapter. The daily amount of time you dedicate to writing the e-book will also determine how long it is going to take you to complete it. If you're writing the e-book with the hope of gaining monetarily, you must know that it will probably take several months or even years before you can start gaining any profit from the e-book. For you to become a successful author, you should spend several hours each day working on the e-book.

You should also be prepared to commit significant amounts of cash if you're thinking of writing an e-book. For instance, you'll have to spend some money when doing research about the e-book. If you're doing online or face to face interviews, you might be forced to hire a professional research firm. If you're thinking of collecting information from a large geographical region, you'll probably spend huge sums of money traversing the vast area. The only way you can become a successful author is if you're ready and willing to set aside significant amounts of money for the project.

Once you have enough cash and time, nothing should force you to abandon the project. You can start writing the e-book and continue up to the last chapter. While writing it, try to stick to the title and topics that you want to write about. After all, the reader will buy the book after looking at the title and topics. Why waste their time covering a different agenda from what is listed on the title and topics?

Regardless of your level of accuracy, you will probably make several errors while typing the e-book. This means that as soon as you're through with typing it, you have to read it and edit the obvious mistakes. After the first editing, you will still have to go through it several times while looking at sentence structure and grammatical mistakes. After you've proofread it several times, you need to let other people-probably your friends- go through it and pinpoint mistakes if there are any. The next step is to hire a professional proofreader to fine-tune the document and get rid of all mistakes if there are any. Once the proofreader is done, you can use software designed to point out grammatical and spelling errors in a word document. There are several websites that offer this software conveniently and at affordable rates. You should also ensure that you've not plagiarized anybody's work. If there are no errors after running the e-book through the software, you can go ahead and publish it.

Alternatively you can decide to hire a professional publishing firm after you've written the e-book. The main advantage of hiring a publishing firm is that you won't spend a lot of time editing and formatting the e-book. The publisher will have to edit the e-book and correct all mistakes. The publisher should also ensure that you've not plagiarized anybody's work. With a publisher, all that you'll do is write the e-book and then hand it over to them. They'll then take it from there and do everything else up to the point where the book will be ready for sale. Unlike when you self-publish the e-book, you will have to use extra resources if you're thinking of enlisting the services of a publishing firm. You therefore have to consider the money in your bank before deciding whether to hire a professional publishing firm or self-publish the book.

While preparing the e-book for publishing, you have to ensure that it is highly protected and can only be accessed by those who have to or need to access it. You'll be very disappointed if somebody steals your ideas and writes his/her own book about the same ideas before you've published it. It is also possible that somebody might steal the document and publish it as his/her own. After all, how can you prove that you're the rightful owner of the document? Rather than wait to be disappointed, why not ensure that the book can't be accessed by unauthorized people before it is published.

After you've written the e-book, you still need to protect it from counterfeiting. The only way you can do so is by including security features that can be used to distinguish the genuine e-books from fakes. There are several companies that specialize in security features for books and hence it is up to you to identify the one with a good reputation. Remember that anti-counterfeiting features are not only applicable for hardcopies of books but also for softcopies (e-books).

What You Must Never Do When Writing E-Books

There are several things that you must never do if you're keen on becoming an expert at writing e-books. Some of these things might land you in jail or result in a very poor quality e-book. If you're not very careful, you may end-up writing an e-book that nobody will ever bother to read. The following are some of the things that you must never do if you want to succeed in writing e-books:

- Writing about outdated topics, procedures or ideas

While identifying the topics and titles to include in an e-book, you should try imagining that you're the reader. Can you really spend your cash to purchase it and then take your time to read it? If the answer is 'NO', you have no option but to write about something else. Suppose you came across a book that explains how to fix a vacuum tube TV, can you read it? All electronic companies stopped manufacturing such TVs several decades ago. Even if you read an e-book about vacuum tube TVs it won't help you in any way. The only way you can become a successful author is by writing about modern technology and currently trending topics.

- Write about something you don't understand

You should also never make the mistake of writing an e-book about a topic that you don't understand or like. If you write such an e-book, you'll probably make several mistakes or even give inaccurate information. If you have to write the e-book, just make sure that you have done thorough research and collected information from as many sources as possible.

- Poor English and unedited books

For you to write helpful books and build a good reputation, you must ensure that you're fluent in English. If English is not your first language, you will probably have to spend several months in a country where English is widely spoken. This way you'll get to have a larger vocabulary and a deeper understanding of the language. You must also never publish a poorly edited e-book. Assuming you're the reader, can you buy a book from an author whose other books are poorly edited and contain several mistakes?

- Incoherency in flow of ideas

Regardless of the genre of e-book, you must always ensure that the ideas discussed in the e-book flow naturally and coherently. Coherency is all about the chronological order in which ideas appear in the e-book. If for example you're writing about historical events, you might want to start with the oldest events and then finish with the newest event. Once the reader starts reading the e-book, he/she should be able to understand the e-book as he/she is reading it.

- Making assumptions instead of getting clarification

Before writing anything, you must ensure that you have all the facts and information about the topic. This means that you should never assume that you know the meaning of a given phrase, sentence or paragraph. If there is ambiguity in your source of information, you better clarify it by consulting experts or the author.

- Using words and phrases whose meanings you don't know

While writing an e-book you might be tempted to use words whose meanings you know vaguely or don't understand at all. However, you should never make this mistake as you might end up delivering a totally different message from what you intended. Ensure that you have a softcopy or hardcopy dictionary while writing the e-book. This way you can easily find the meaning of any word before using it in the e-book.

Conclusion

With dedication, hard-work and perseverance, writing an e-book will be the easiest thing that you can ever do. You just have to start working on the ideas in this book and soon you'll be one of the most successful authors. You don't have to write just one e-book and then give up. If other people have managed to juggle between their busy schedules and write several e-books, why not you?

The task of writing an e-book is even easier if you've already published another one in the past. This is because you'll know exactly how to identify the topics and tittles, the sources of information, what to do and what not to do.

Start your journey to becoming an experienced and renowned e-books author by considering the ideas discussed in the book "How to Become an Expert at writing e-books."

Author Bio

Colvin Tonya Nyakundi

Colvin Tonya Nyakundi is a freelance writer and co-author of 'How to Become an Expert at Writing E-books' Apart from that book, he has a portfolio of several other publications accumulated in the more than two years that he has been freelancing through www.odesk.com.

He has authored several personal relationships, construction and real estate, lifestyle and travel and holiday guide publications. Other books that he has co-authored include 'How to Survive in the Woods', 'How to Start Making Money Online', 'How to Survive in a Desert', 'How to Improve Your Communication Skills,' 'Construction Guide for New Investors in Real Estate,' 'How to Make Your Backyard a Magnificent Venue for Hosting Events', 'How to Identify the Perfect Holiday Destination', "How Your Favorite Meal Could be Killing You Slowly" and 'How to Prepare and Survive in a Foreign Country.' You can get in touch with him through his official Facebook account, tonyanc@facebook.com.

Our books are available at

1. Amazon.com
2. Barnes and Noble
3. Itunes
4. Kobo
5. Smashwords
6. Google Play Books

Check out some of the other JD-Biz Publishing books

Gardening Series on Amazon

Health Learning Series

Country Life Books

Health Learning Series

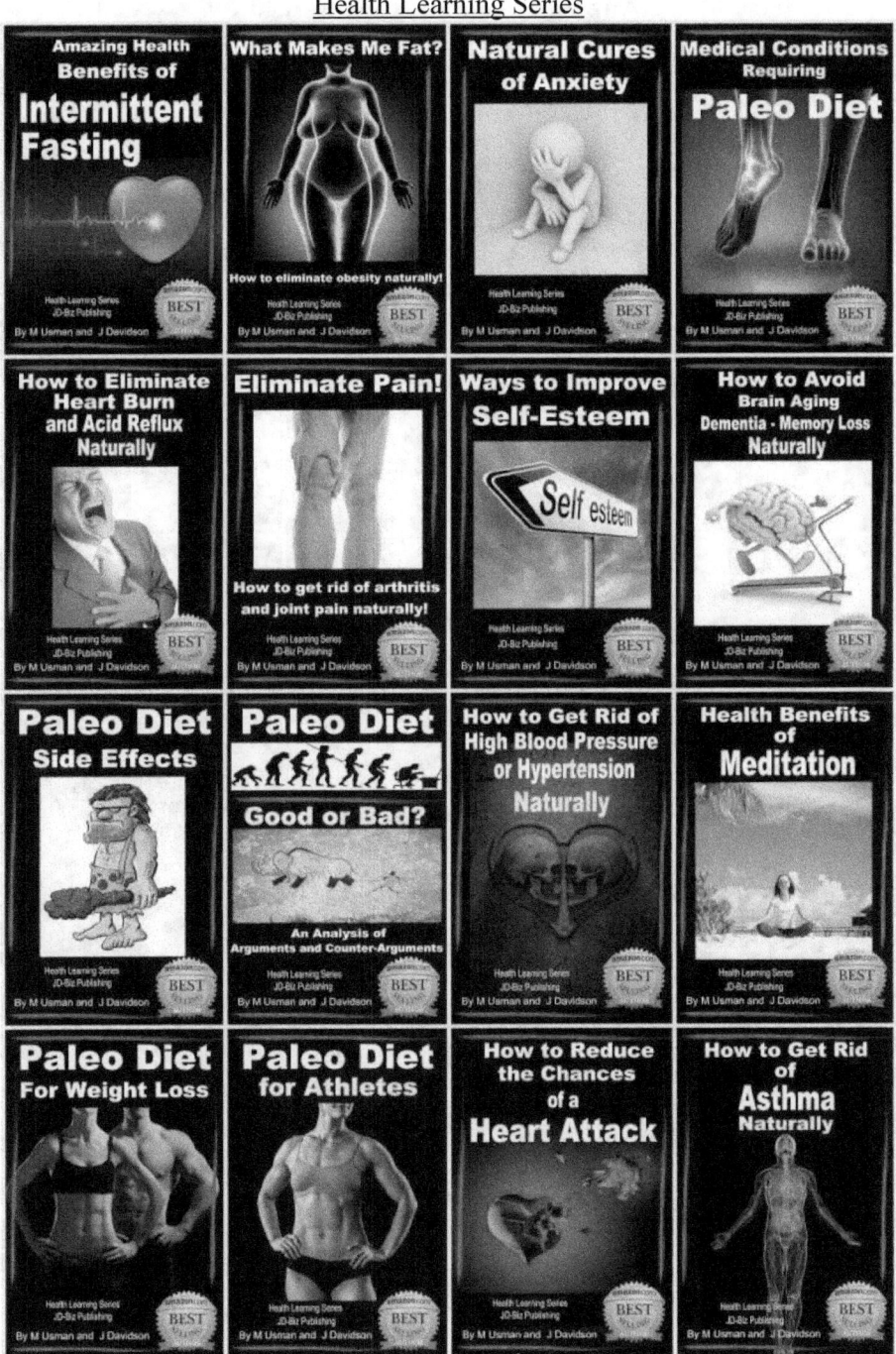

How to Build and Plan Books

Publisher

JD-Biz Corp

P O Box 374

Mendon, Utah 84325

http://www.jd-biz.com/